j994
Cobb

IMAGINE LIVING HERE

THIS PLACE IS
LONELY

By
Vicki Cobb

Illustrated by
Barbara Lavallee

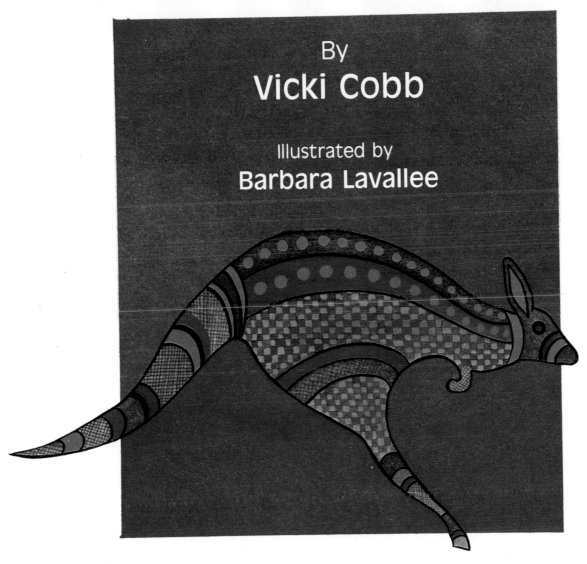

Walker and Company
New York

The author and illustrator gratefully acknowledge the help of the following people: Lindsay Smith, Helen Styles, Jim Stein, and Diane Lilley of the Australian Overseas Information Service; Andrew Sinclair of Queensland Tourist and Travel Corporation; Dr. Barry Richardson and Alex George of the Australian Bureau of Flora and Fauna; Peter W. Lynch of the Division of Wildlife and Ecology; Ian Meek of the Australian National Parks and Wildlife Service; Brenda Hodgkinson and Jeanette Andrews of the Broken Hill School of the Air; Vicki and Bob Seekamp and their children, Tara, Tim, and Angus, of Woolcunda Station, NSW; Max Bourke of the Australia Council for the Arts; Mary Joyce of Magnetic North Tourism Authority; Kathy Sharrett of Colonial Gardens Resort, Townsville, QLD; Ellen Collins of Down Under Tours, QLD; Rober Prette-john of the Kewarra Beach Resort, QLD; Tony Cope and Alex Wildenborg-Hammarskold.

First published in the United States of America in 1991
by Walker Publishing Company, Inc.

Published simultaneously in Canada by Thomas Allen & Son
Canada, Limited, Markham, Ontario

Library of Congress Cataloging-in-Publication Data

Cobb, Vicki.
This place is lonely / by Vicki Cobb; illustrated by Barbara Lavalle.
p.   cm. — (Imagine living here)
Summary: Presents Australia as a possible place to live,
mentioning that though you may "go to school" by radio, it has other
good features.
ISBN 0-8027-6959-4. — ISBN 0-8027-6960-8 (lib. bdg.)
1. Australia—Description and travel— 1981- —Juvenile literature.
2. Country life—Australia—Juvenile literature. (1. Australia—
Description and travel.) I. Lavalle, Barbara, ill. II. Title.
III. Series: Cobb, Vicki. Imagine living here.
DU105.2.C63   1990
994.06'3—dc20   90-11997   CIP   AC

Printed in Hong Kong

2 4 6 8 10 9 7 5 3 1

If you lived on the outback of Australia, the only people you would see every day would be your own family. Your nearest neighbor might be fifty miles away or more. You would have to get along with your brothers and sisters, or you would have no one to play with. A visit to friends or going shopping would be overnight trips. Very few people live in the huge interior of Australia, known as the outback or the "bush." Most Australians live in cities along the eastern and southern coasts of their island continent.

The usual outback family business is raising sheep or cattle. Ranches are called "stations" and are very big. If you lived on the outback, your family might have an airplane to find the livestock that roams freely on your land. To most of us, life on a sheep or cattle station seems lonely.

The outback is dotted with patches of grass and shrubs. Even if irrigation was possible, the soil is too salty for most crops. The plants can be food for grazing animals, but in some places the outback is such poor pasture land that the plants on fourteen acres are only enough for one sheep. That's why a mid-sized station with eight thousand sheep is two hundred square miles.

Station managers have to make sure that there is always enough water for their animals. Here and there on their property, station managers place tanks to catch rainwater or build wind-driven pumps to bring up well water for their livestock.

Although the average rainfall on the outback is ten inches a year, you can't count on getting that amount every year. It's possible to get forty inches one year, all of it falling in one month, and then have no rain for the next three years. Not too long ago, an area of the outback got so much rain that in one day a lake appeared that had not existed for over fifty years!

All stations are built to collect whatever rain does fall. This caught water is called "catchment." The station house, the airplane hangar, and all other station buildings have roofs made of grooved iron sheets. Rainwater runs down the grooves into gutters that lead to tanks. From the tanks, the catchment water is pumped into the house. People try to save water. The tap is not running when teeth are brushed, bath water may be shared by the family, there are no dishwashers (they use too much water), and the toilets have a half-flush and a full-flush, depending on how much waste you need to get rid of.

Many stations are too remote to get electricity from public utilities that supply towns. It is very expensive to string wire for miles into the outback for just one home. People make their own electricity with noisy generators that burn diesel fuel. Every so often, a station gets a fuel delivery for its generators and vehicles.

Mail is delivered once a week by a bush pilot. The mailman may bring fresh fruits and vegetables from town, as well as the latest gossip.

Telephone wires are also rare on the outback. Some stations that are not too far from a town have telephones. More and more stations are turning to wireless telephone service using satellites. But all stations have two-way radios. Radios use radio waves, a kind of light energy, to send and receive messages. The radio was once called a ``wireless'' because it sent and received messages without wires.

The radio is important in the outback, especially in emergencies. You can't call an ambulance in the outback, but you can radio the Royal Flying Doctor Service or RFDS. The RFDS has a fleet of small planes that are equipped like ambulances. A pilot and doctor respond immediately to a call for help. The Flying Doctor pilots are skilled at landing on station landing strips, many of which are nothing more than a cleared dirt path on the bush. Before the RFDS was established in the 1920s, people in isolated areas who were ill or in an accident often died before help could arrive. Today there are several Flying Doctor centers throughout the outback. Thanks to the two-way radio, no station is more than two hours away from medical help.

The radio is also important to children on the outback. They use it to go to their school, the School of the Air. At 9:00 on school days, all the children from kindergarten to sixth grade are at their radios for morning assembly. They hear messages from the principal and some of their teachers who are in a broadcasting studio. They sing the school song. In order to speak or sing over the radio, you have to push a button on your microphone to transmit the message. When you are finished, you say "over" and push another button so that you could hear your teacher. When your teacher finishes she says, "over." Unlike a telephone, which can receive and transmit at the same time, you have to take turns on the radio. So if you had a part in a school play, you would put on your costume and say your lines on the radio while your family watched. When you were finished with a line, you'd say "over." You would have to imagine the rest of the players on a stage.

A corner of your home is set up as your school area. During the day, you might have two or three forty-five-minute radio classes with a small group in your grade. You receive your lessons and books and video-tapes in the weekly mail. Schoolwork is mailed in to be graded. Once a year, your teacher pays a visit to your station. Twice a year you meet for a two-day workshop with classmates in your area at someone's station. It is a great sleep-over party, sometimes called a ``galah'' after a noisy, silly Australian parrot.

If you lived on the outback, you would spend a lot of time outdoors. At night, the stars are especially bright because the air is so clear and dry and there are no city lights to make the stars appear dim. Several of the world's most important observatories and satellite tracking stations are located here.

During the day, you would get to know some of the amazing animals that live only in Australia.

The *emu* (E-moo) is the largest bird in Australia and the second largest bird in the world after the African ostrich. It is between five and six feet tall and can weigh up to 120 pounds. Like the ostrich, it cannot fly, but it can run as fast as forty miles an hour. In the 1930s, station managers in Western Australia declared a "war" on the emus because they were breaking down fences and trampling grain. The station managers tried to herd the birds into flocks and shoot them with machine guns. But the birds scattered and only a few were killed. Since that time, research has shown that emus eat caterpillars that can destroy crops, so it's a good thing the emus won the war!

The second largest bird in Australia is a close relative of the emu called the *cassowary* (CAS-so-worry). It has a bony growth on the top of its head that protects it as it runs head down through the jungle. Like the emus, the female cassowaries lay their eggs, the males are the ones who spend weeks sitting on them until they hatch.

Kangaroos grazing on grass are a common sight on the outback. Since grazing animals eat with their heads down, they can be taken unaware by their enemies. Evolution has protected the kangaroos by giving them large movable ears to pick up the sounds of predators. They also have eyes with long, horizontal pupils on the sides of their heads that give them a wide view.

The kangaroo's head is almost exactly the same as the head of a mule deer that lives in the American southwest. Similar appearances and living habits of unrelated living things that help them survive similar conditions is called "convergent evolution."

The similarity between the kangaroo and the mule deer ends with the head. Kangaroos are the only large animals on earth that move by hopping on strong, large hind legs. Believe it or not, hopping in great bounds uses less energy than running on four legs at the same speed. Large red kangaroos have been clocked moving at about forty miles an hour and can leap more than twelve feet with each bound. Males will also use their large hind legs as weapons when they fight each other over a female.

Another unusual thing about kangaroos is the way they reproduce. A kangaroo is a mammal—an animal that feeds milk to, or nurses, its babies. Most mammals give birth to a fully formed baby that has been nourished inside its mother's womb. But a kangaroo, which can weigh over one hundred pounds, gives birth to a baby that weighs only a few ounces and is only about one inch long. It is pink, hairless, and blind, and has undeveloped hind legs. At birth, it crawls with its forelimbs about three inches through its mother's fur to a pouch on the mother's belly. Once inside the pouch, the tiny kangaroo latches onto a nipple. It becomes so firmly attached for the next few months that it can't be disconnected without injury to its mouth or the nipple. When it is about six months old, the joey, as the baby kangaroo is now called, makes short trips out of its mother's pouch to learn to eat grass. It still jumps back in headfirst when it is frightened and will continue to nurse until it is about a year old.

Mammals with pouches are called *marsupials* (mar-SOUP-ee-als). The only marsupial in North America is the opossum. But in Australia, marsupials are the main kind of mammal. There are marsupial types for many of the kinds of mammals you know, including marsupial mice, moles, cats, and wolves. And, of course, there are marsupials that are completely different from familiar mammals.

One very popular marsupial is the slow, sleepy koala. Perhaps it is so well-liked because it looks like a cuddly teddy bear. During the day, the koalas sleep in the forked branches of *eucalyptus* (you-cah-lipt-us) or ``gum'' trees. Eucalyptuses are one of the most common of all Australian trees. At night, koalas they eat the leaves of their home. The oily leaves of eucalyptus are all they eat. The leaves have a pepperminty flavor and are thought to contain some chemicals that make koalas sleepy.

Some other interesting marsupials are the sugar gliders and squirrel gliders. Distant cousins of opossums, they have extra skin along their sides that act as wings. They can move in gliding leaps of more than three hundred feet from tree to tree without touching the ground, where an enemy might turn them into a meal. The seventy-pound wombat builds the largest burrow in the world. Some of its tunnels can be sixty feet long. Bandicoots feed at night, eating plants, insects, and meat. They are very faithful to their own feeding area, even if it happens to be an open-air restaurant.

Imagine an animal that has fur like an otter, a bill like a duck, a tail like a beaver, and clawed, webbed feet good for both swimming and digging burrows. It lays eggs like a reptile but feeds milk to its babies like a mammal. No, it is not a joke. This creature is called a platypus, a name that means "flat-foot." It is a kind of primitive mammal known as a monotreme, meaning "one hole." Monotremes have a single opening in their bodies for getting rid of waste and for laying eggs.

There is only one other monotreme on earth and it, too, lives in Australia. It's called the *echidna* (ah-kid-na), also known as the spiny anteater. It has spines all over its body for protection, like a hedgehog. The female curls her body so that she can lay her egg in a pouch that has developed two days earlier on her belly. After a week or so, the egg hatches and the baby nurses on milk that runs into the pouch from the mother's belly. It stays in the pouch for about seven weeks until it starts getting spines.

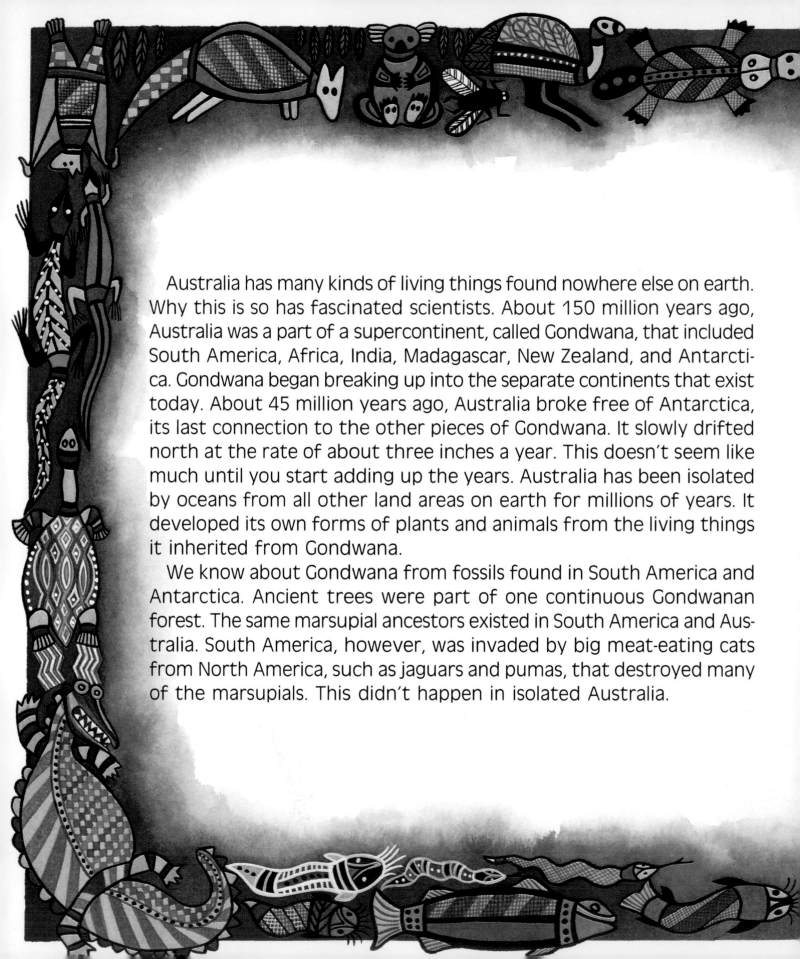

Australia has many kinds of living things found nowhere else on earth. Why this is so has fascinated scientists. About 150 million years ago, Australia was a part of a supercontinent, called Gondwana, that included South America, Africa, India, Madagascar, New Zealand, and Antarctica. Gondwana began breaking up into the separate continents that exist today. About 45 million years ago, Australia broke free of Antarctica, its last connection to the other pieces of Gondwana. It slowly drifted north at the rate of about three inches a year. This doesn't seem like much until you start adding up the years. Australia has been isolated by oceans from all other land areas on earth for millions of years. It developed its own forms of plants and animals from the living things it inherited from Gondwana.

We know about Gondwana from fossils found in South America and Antarctica. Ancient trees were part of one continuous Gondwanan forest. The same marsupial ancestors existed in South America and Australia. South America, however, was invaded by big meat-eating cats from North America, such as jaguars and pumas, that destroyed many of the marsupials. This didn't happen in isolated Australia.

Scientists are not sure exactly when the first people, called *aborigines* (a-bor-IG-in-ees), arrived in Australia. They think they may have come from New Guinea about forty thousand years ago. Aborigines were wanderers who hunted and gathered food. They used fire to drive animals out of the forest and then killed them as they escaped. Aborigines also used fire to clear the land to make traveling easier. Over the years they learned how to use different plants and animals for food, medicine, clothing, tools, musical instruments, and art.

The aborigines tell stories of how their land came to be in legends known as the Dreamtime. In the Dreamtime, people and nature are part of each other. There are holy places, called Dreaming sites, where the great spirits of the Dreamtime still live. These spirits are celebrated in aboriginal art that has been painted on rock walls. Aboriginal paintings often show the insides of animals as if they were x-rayed.

It's hard to believe that an island continent as large as Australia was only guessed about by Europeans for centuries. By the eighteenth century, navigators from Europe knew how to sail long distances and there were well-established trade routes between Europe and the East Indies. But Australia didn't have any of the riches other countries wanted. It was so far away that it was expensive to send ships there without some payoff.

In August 1768, England's famous Captain James Cook set off on a voyage in his ship, the *Endeavour*, that would finally put the east coast of Australia on the map. After a year and a half of sailing, he sighted the southeast coast of Australia and sailed north for nine days until he finally found a safe harbor. He named the site Botany Bay because a botanist aboard his ship named Joseph Banks found so many new and strange plants there. One group of plants, famous for their large spiky flowers, are called "banksias" in his honor.

The *Endeavour* continued its journey up the coast. After five weeks it entered waters between the shoreline to the west and a huge, dangerous underwater reef to the east. Today we know the reef as the Great Barrier Reef, the rocky creation of billions of tiny sea animals called corals that form structures of limestone in warm, shallow sea water. Today, snorkelers and scuba divers marvel at the beautiful corals and the many kinds of sea creatures that live on the reef. But for Captain Cook, the Great Barrier Reef was nothing but trouble. The *Endeavour* hit the reef, tearing a gaping hole in the hull that took seven weeks to repair. The Great Barrier Reef has caused at least two hundred other wrecks over the years.

In 1788, a British fleet of eleven ships arrived in Botany Bay to establish a colony there. It wasn't to be an ordinary town, but a prison. The ships held about one thousand people, three-quarters of whom were convicts. The colony they started is now Sydney, Australia.

Early colonists found life in Australia tough going. Captain Cook's crew had seen the area in the fall at its best, right after the short rainy season. The colonists were not prepared for the dry conditions and had trouble growing crops. They depended on ships to bring them supplies, but the long distances to Australia meant that supply ships were few and far between. For the first few years they nearly starved.

Some of the animals people brought with them have become wild in Australia.

About three thousand years ago, a kind of dog, called the dingo, appeared in Australia. It must have been brought here by the aborigines. The dingo, a meat-eater, found marsupials easy prey. It also found many other things it liked to eat, including insects and lizards. The dingo thrived and multiplied so fast that it became a pest to later settlers, particularly to sheep farmers. Dingoes killed off many lambs. There was no way the farmers could kill off the dingoes, so the government built a six thousand mile-long fence called the "Dog Fence" to keep dingoes out of sheep country. It is the longest fence in the world and has done its job fairly well.

Over the past two hundred years, settlers from other lands brought domestic animals that have become feral or wild. Rabbits were first brought to Australia to be raised for food. Feral rabbits spread around Australia so rapidly that they became a plague, eating crops and digging burrows that destroyed the best farmland. Camels were brought to help build a railroad across the desert. Herds of feral camels now range over the desert. Feral cats and feral pigs thrive in the Australian countryside.

Isolation from the rest of the world has kept Australia free from certain animal and plant diseases. As a result, Australia has some of the strictest laws in the world about bringing living things into the country. For example, all airplanes are sprayed to kill foreign insects before landing in Australia. And pet dogs from foreign countries must be held in isolation for a total of nine months to make sure they are free of disease before they can live in Australia.

Australia is a melting pot of people from many lands. The art and legends of the aborigines have made a strong impression on modern Australia. Australia is far away, but airplane travel and television make it a part of the modern world. A short trip from any Australian city can take you to unspoiled country where you are close to nature and where you can enjoy being alone—without feeling lonely. Most visitors find that it's easy to imagine living here.